Indelicate Sundays

larrahteasdale6@gmail.com

Previous Poetry Collections,

Laid Bare
Hannah M. Teasdale
(2016, Burning Eye)

Milked
Thommie Gillow and Hannah Teasdale
(2018, Burning Eye)

Indelicate Sundays

HANNAH M. TEASDALE

Black Eyes Publishing UK

Indelicate Sundays
© HANNAH M. TEASDALE, 2023

First published in 2023
Black Eyes Publishing UK
Gloucester
United Kingdom

www.blackeyespublishinguk.co.uk

ISBN: 978-1-913195-25-0

Edited by: Josephine Lay

Cover: Jason Conway, The Daydream Academy
             www.thedaydreamacademy.com

Cover picture: Hannah M. Teasdale

Contents

Part 1

Part 2

Part 3

Part 1

The Night

she said we were leaving
Band Aid was feeding the world.

Geldof slurred pixelated pleas
from the corner of my nine-year-old mind.

We sat around the kitchen table
the four of us, knees brushing.

Cutlery, a bright distraction
from pork chops, carrots and potato

mashed with frustration and control.
She wore ten years of strain

like high-street foundation, rose-tinted
flashes slapped across each cheek.

The Heirloom

You hack his chest apart
I watch from the bathroom window
my forty-five-degree view slashed
through frosted glass. Your sweat
spatters the splintered pine
and smudges the inky scrawl
of misspelt words – rebellion of the female
neither of us know. My final piece
of him is now shredded. Afterwards
in the wet and whisper of night-time
I stack the timber to fill
the carcass of the strongest drawer.
Our grey neighbour likes to forage
on Sunday mornings for firewood.

This weekend, I give him a gift.

Mother

you crouch
at the water's edge
head hung like a convict
on the run. A vague drizzle breaks
your reflection. As inconsistent
as the weather, sunlight masks
you like the sheath of a forced
smile. Your tears bead
in the tide that flows
to the silt-filth depth of oceans
where your skewed lips
first found life.

Layers

We have a room
where we lie together
through each frozen night
wearing tracksuit bottoms, two pairs

of socks, extra blankets, jumpers, hats.
I can always see my breath
through the twilight.
But often, I don't see yours.

Panda lies face down
suffocating in your absence
strands of your hair stick to his button eyes.
He feels dead

when in hope, I stroke him
back into sleep.
We are frozen
without our patchwork blanket.

Indelicate Sunday

We arrive

You pour

One drink

Eyes catch

My daddy

Dim light

I fall

In half

Once again

Matthew

Lemon Curd kid
with your sallow skin
and dirty smile, I see yours
as you see mine.

We kiss our teddies
soft heads held steady
somersault from the mattress
in my frozen room

we carve the polystyrene tiles
on the ceiling
and leave ourselves
in traces

like a snow angel
I take the fall
nothing left
to lose.

The Hobby

I was around nine –
my first desire
to take things that aren't mine.
Not from real people
from whom it counts.
I never take more
than I feel owed.

Within a month of us leaving
I've built a collection
of eclectic items:
incense holders from
'Pottery and Pieces', magazines
from the newsagent – full of tits and cunts
(fuck knows how I even reach them)
shoelaces wrapped in plastic
Wrigley's spearmint gum
'on offer' to store
in my Coronation tin
under our filthy bed
untouched

until guilt ravages me
through the night. The only way
to straighten my head
is to put things back
in different places.

Shrunken in your shadow

I place incense sticks
between cheese slices
in Tesco and hand out
penny chews to fellow Gnomes
at Brownies
(the Oxfam charity collection –
I help myself to)

All I keep
is a pack of Polos
habitually inspected, to curl
around my little fingers,
to sniff and lick.

I have some Tic-Tacs too
to pop when things get bad
like Mother does.
But it never stops.

By thirteen, I have
reams of knickers and
M&S bras I cannot fill.
The High Street makes it
far too easy; Saturday's favourite:
the Jelly Bean Stand in BHS.
Convinced I am not stealing
if I can linger
in the aisles to eat them.

Knee High

With a sock full of marbles
I chance my hand
from a collection of Tiddlers
and Grandpa's single ball-bearing
worth ten-to-one. After school
against the boys
I win every game and lose
potential friends.

Driving

We suck the silence
between us, from the Fisherman's Friends
kept in the glove compartment
in moments that stretch
like the elastic bands at each end
of my carefully constructed plaits.

The music keeps playing
track after tear-convincing track.
I hear, 'If leaving me is easy'
as the motorway spans either side of us.

And he says nothing until he drops
me home, other than:

'Remember to tell your mother that.'

My Mouth

always feels too small for my face
until I look at photographs. Then I see

how it spreads through my face and I wonder
how anything can stay inside it. But things do

I know. They stay closed up, gnawed, chewed
by my even more enormous teeth – the reason

I am called 'Bugs Bunny' in the playground
with wires that rip the pink-soft flesh but keep

my secrets from spilling out. But they do spill
sometimes, in the middle of the night

when it seems, there is no one left to hear. Me –
I don't speak anymore. I just let the silence

fall into the crevices of memories. And then worry
how easily my mind weaves blanks into lies.

I open my mouth
So loud are these words that speak
only in my head.

Lego house

I build a Lego house
on her short-changed breasts –
small disruption to the pieces
of green and red, red and green
stuck
on top of one another
stacked
over
and over

until my skinny fingers
hunting through the box
deafens us
and I am plucked
from the warm patch
of blue hospital blanket
and told to say
'Goodbye.'

Afterwards, we stand outside
the rain pelting
like war. I pretend
not to notice Mother's tears
beneath the last-minute umbrella.
The bus stops
and I ask, 'Is Granny dead?'

She turns away from me
and pays our fare.

She is Nowhere

This Helena, I found as a child
when I knew her
in the wispy-damp house, where fog lay
blankets across the boards

of the top floor
stacks of naked rooms
less the frightening art
propped on windowsills

that repelled me. All macabre
but one in particular
I could never stop seeing.
At night, I climbed

as she lay in her bed
staring upwards at the creak
of me above; ghostly
as the whitening of her eyes

not seen in the folds
of twice-lined curtains
nor hanging from the edge
of the bathroom mirror.

Not thrown by the strip
of landing light stretched
across the bedroom floor
nor a stool-height-catch

beneath an empty wine glass
in a room without seats
or spare drinks.
I shut my eyes and imagine

the spin of her fresh web
inside the tin
candy-floss caged
under the bed.

The sheets where she slept
smell eleven years old
Stained linen, still fresh.

The Wake

A corner of cucumber
hangs limp
like her lips did yesterday.
Glued together, cold as Winter's dawn
her skin, wilted like the baby spinach
discarded at the back of our fridge.

We do not like the gown;
alkaline satin ribbons
with white piped frosting
teased at the edges

like wedding cake: her hollow
face pops through the middle.
And where did her eyelashes go?
We know polyester burns
ferociously, like sugar.

Glass Eyes

The black of the attic spills
across our lids. I imagine almost
anything; the doll's glass eyes
fixed like lenses on tripods

the rise and fall of your buttocks –
every other second forbidden
territory coming in to focus.
Her porcelain feet resting

at the window's edge, shadow-less
as the new moon sheds
blue light on our kaleidoscope
of greys. Your luminous scent

fills me in wave after wave; yet
I think of nothing but the secrets
hidden beneath the unearthly
mask of her ceramic gaze.

Tumbling

It is not easy
to anticipate the feeling;
reminiscent of a run-up to the vault.
A gymnast's dread
to throw your body
through the unknown.

Head might spin
the wrong way
a blank page, my crash mat.
I cannot risk to tumble.

Nobody warned me
it would ever feel
like this.

The Inheritance

I sit at my Magic Roundabout
plastic gratitude
fills the room.
Dougal lies upside down
Zebedee looks
strung out.

The carousel doesn't turn.
I try to remember
how to play
whilst the Yorkshire puddings
forget to rise
and Grandpa can't stop

burping through adult conversation.
I forget the name
of my favourite character
the one with a shock of black hair
and foolish shoes
I know Grandpa doesn't know.

Everyone has to have a name
so, I make up a story
about how she decided
just last night
it was better to be dead.

Underlay

I sit at the landing, in dim light
straining to listen – still
guilt-ridden by my ear-wigging.
An adult louse drops in
uninvited by the cracks
in my own window sill.

I can't come down
can't be seen. I can only shrivel
amongst the frays in the carpet pile
smothered by the stale years
soaked into our underlay
at the top of my stairs.

Untouched

The day folds itself in half, then half again.
Clouds knit themselves together
squeezing the final blues from sight.

Gloom blossoms in bruised greys
beneath her eyes and in the rest
of the two crimson slits –

her miserable wound of a mouth.
I watch the drops spatter from different sources
and cling to the closeness in the air that hangs

in drapes between us. The window remains
untouched – small reflections quiver
like pond life. She has nothing lovely to say.

Later, I open the box, and it comes to me
in a flurry of pieces; remnants
of that closed-fist punch of land:

cufflinks, badges, a grandfather's wrist watch –
clocking hard-eyed streets where Winter choked
in miles of plastic shoes and propositions.

The night throws an odd light, illuminating
from the open window, the deep rivets
stretching her difficult face.

The Morning

she says we are leaving
I had begun to butter my toast.

It is just the two of us; her torso wedged
at the back door. She always exhales

cigarette smoke through her nose. I feel bad
for my brown breakfast and ensure every inch

wears an even blanket of yellow, before hiding
it behind the bin. We have an hour, she says

to pack and clean. Time gets lost somewhere
and the only thing I remember

is the empty Coronation tin
hidden beneath my single bed.

Part 2

Circa 1917

I look at his picture
through the eyes of my sixteen
year-old self and feel the flutter
between my legs. Straight-backed
shades of grey depict a warrior-lust
in both him and me. He, eighteen –
freshly-pressed uniform yet to be stained
with virgin's blood. I stand
knickers damp at my grandfather's
mantelpiece whilst he burps
through Sunday lunch. His bowels
relaxing now his wife
is two year's dead.

Predicting the Weather

I saw you, crouched at the water's edge
head hung like a convict on the run.

The slant rain breaking your own reflection.
Inconsistent as the weather; an hour earlier

the sun broke through like the shards
of our forced smiles, and your tears – drops

in the inevitable tides that flow to the depths
of oceans where this dirty rain first found life.

This yellow dress disarms you, confused
by how pretty my skin looks.

I am nineteen and childless, wearing a plan
like it is something I was born with.

Your cheeks flush with a hot, brief ease
as you realise how yellow cannot suit me.

The arch of my back
hides our everything beneath
crushing buttercups

Happy Hour

The way you hold her
at the bar, I'd think you'd been missing
for at least a decade; the limpet-grip
leeching each breath
from your lungs. It smells
of murder – stings my eyes
sucks particles from my skin.
She clings like humidity
from your shoulders.

This place blazes of 'steak-night'
onion ring circles served amongst
their heat. She looks half-starved –
chomping mouths, a cacophony
of applause. Then feet fall
towards discarded beer mats
she reaches behind you to snatch
her empty wine glass and returns
to the only vacant stool at the bar.

Handbook of Gloss-Rich Pleasure

I run on hollow
sketch my way
through everyone
else's picture frames

I separate from you
by my ribcage – the gaps
not quite wide enough
to reach through

our zero-sized prisoner
hindered by a brittle mirror
and set of scales where I balance
each foot off the record.

Hungry Romance

In Spring
we made love on your father's grave.
You left bite-marks
replacements for my bra-straps.

In Summer
you said nothing to the farmer
whose berries you pierced the middles through
on your quest for the ultimate pick-your-own.

On birthdays
you were anonymous and on Valentine's, you left.
You bought yourself a watch for Christmas
and forgot to book the table by the fire.

You always left me hungry
I tattooed your mouth inside my thigh.
You never knew the meaning
why I bit my tongue when you spoke.

Wrapped Up

I remember you like yesterday
like last Christmas:
the clear difficulty of said words
          few meant, most not –
                    all engraved in memory.

The feeling of anticipation
tinged with predictable
despair
          in hope the next unwraps
                    with more ease.

Though experience adorns
the futile with gold
bands and blushes red ribbons.

Complex Compounds

Braised in our own juices
sweat-drenched in patchouli, tobacco smoke
and worn pages of Penguin Classics
we caught our small exchange of air.

I almost said it then
last night
when we were deep inside
one another. Though I think
you already knew; hands
sliding the length of you
ribs interlocking – different
pieces of the same puzzle.

Your pupils bloomed before I found you
at the edge, slightly wilted.
I imagined my own birth, tightened
my grip, closed my eyes
and imagined I could shrink the sky.

Twisting toes into new moulds
we swelled to twice our size.

The sheets where we lay
and created twice of us
were stained when you left.

The Weir

Let's try our luck at getting lost
and step out into the slant-rain, black

storm the path where rivers flood
and chip-wrappers, dog-shit and lichen

become one. Let us locate ourselves, or not
by the water's flow, upstream, from the bank

where his bloated body was found. They think
he didn't mean to drown, local chatter hinting

he was pushed by a gang of junkie tramps
a good story. I push down my jeans, squat. Piss

behind an emergency life ring. Your clothing fades
into nowhere and my downstream disappears.

The Three-Legged Dog in Downtown, New Orleans

I know I shouldn't be here; I smell it
in the dirty silence. This district burns

beneath its surface; vast wasteland
where lush reeds, blades of emerald swords

slay an atmosphere otherwise bleak.
The punctuation of a disused rail-crossing keeps me

on the same side of the track. Heat climbs
where a sleeping dog lies. Her aged body rises

on three legs, quivering, to sniff my groin.
Headlights against the sunshine find us

tinted windows gauge the outside – the car slows
we meet at stopping distance from my feet

where the matted hound loses interest, and succumbs
to the relief of my shadow. Door opens, a dark shirt

clings to darker skin. He raises his hand, my breath stops
I feel ridiculous – a stereotype of the look behind his lids

as he lifts the frail, grey clatter of skin and bones
and lays it to rest like a corpse upon the back seat.

Pink Taffeta

Though you only noticed blue. Her open mouth
primed like the orchestra we danced to, naked
limbs, an offering to shadow mine. Hanging
in the empty womb of girlhood infatuation
waves of woven silk crashed at dreams. Discarded
debt and crumpled pride left wasted in our eyes.
You said the tone did nothing for my skin.

You are ironed-out, re-attached to the bone-marrow
lining of my fragile, blushing gown. I find my bed
stretch out cramped memories between the sheets
allow the pin-drop silence of this knife-edge
at my side. I cut lines across the mirror
and roll your ticket along my thigh. Snort.
Resolve to never again wear pink.

Man-Made

I stalk there, to the place we once fucked
and feed my demons
with the black sand of memories
that shift between my toes. Salt tears lip
at my peeling skin. I was a virgin
to men like you - selling shares
of time for flesh and bone.
I looked for you
the day after, as disease slid
between my thighs.

Years passed in oceans stretched
across our actions – swabbed
wrapped in rubber life boats
and discounted hotel rooms.
I stalk there, to the place we once fucked
and somewhere past the tumbling distance
I see slivers of us
engraved in the unravel
of volcanic stone.

Ten tied together
hung from my mirror, I watch
our beach crash on glass.

Someone Else's Husband

I need to tell her
that last night I had him
on my sofa – with only the candle
she bought me for Christmas
to shed light

on the situation. I need
to tell her how he teased
my arms from the sleeves
of the cashmere sweater
she bought me from

Debenhams last year. I need
to tell her that I lay beneath
the swaths of cologne she gave him
on Valentine's and how we laughed
at the label, 'patchouli and black pepper'

behind her back on the fifteenth.
I need to tell her how he likes to fill
the vase I bought for their Anniversary
but never shared and how he always
brings Champagne on Sunday nights

when he tells her he's at the gym.
I need to tell her it was me
who persuaded: his growth of a beard
to get his eyes tested and to wear more
navy-blue; black leaves him

pallid – how could she not notice?

Shadow Blank

She cannot let our eyes catch
as Winter light shrinks her
pupils into pins.

Sharp disregard as I stamp
at her face; shadows slide
into my footstep left behind.

Hell-bent to keep stride;
our punctured narrative falls
upon deaf ears.

Through voluminous silence
my name is thrown
like a punch-line.

The Swifts

We were supposed to swallow
Winter. But it was over when
the clocks turned back.

We flew South, faster
than the bubbles burst
on Autumn ground.

A slippery time of year;
leaves cover the exposed
ruins of our nest.

The Storm

I straddle puddles, skirt stretched
above my knees. An outpouring
of tear ducts beneath a skewed umbrella.

Breath ceases to exist here, lungs
drenched as heart cascades to somewhere
just above my feet. There is no view above
only wonderment of what became of us.

I run like print from a page to meet
the cold white hand of a locked
front door where no-one waits behind
to peel the layers to my bones.

Portrait of Lorena Bobbit

It is late July
a thunderstorm breaks
respite from an airless night.
Drivers stop dead
in their tracks, cocooned in tin shelters
under liquid fire.

I watch from the open window
and offer my palms
to the blackened skies
wash my skin of its filthy day.
Steam rises
from the smouldering pavement below.

I go to bed, alone.
Midnight light splays a rainbow
framing pearl-strands of spider-webs.
I drift to sleep
coffee-stained pages
close around my fist.

I wake with breath
at the back of my neck, putrid
from dimly-lit hours drenched
in Jack Daniels and Marlboro Reds.
The swell of you
in tidal waves at my buttocks.

You say you've been out.

Knowing me
to understand
as you catch my wrists.
Fifteen knuckles
knot above my head.

This poem was short-listed for the Gloucestershire Poetry Society 2022 Open Poetry Competition.

Self-Portrait of the Flutter in the Tide

The bare minimum necessary is to survive:
live and wait. Wait to live.

Layers wear away into trenches
full of edges
like the cut pages of a book
water-worn and fretted into lace.

To the gap of shallow
a slight curve of line
a pock interrupts
the pattern of the water, the steep
climb of sea to sky.

Heartbeat visible
like the flutter in the tide.

Air sucks up noise, like scars seal pain –
proof of identity. Blot. Blot. Blot.
Talk into the drift.

Bite yourself.

Egg-shells

Why, when I was a child
could there not have been
bird's eggs
in my bedside drawers?

Meticulously blown by a passionate
father and propped amongst
cotton wool balls and rips
of whimsical tissue.

And the view from the window –
rows of corn rustling
beneath a tangerine sunset, ribbons
of swallows and curious clematis tips?

Not trenches of whores
pinched against a backdrop
of graffitied billboards –
a flirtation of yesterday's news.

I could have caressed their papery shells
with the promise never to shatter them
but to mark my remembrance
with the secret act of uncut fingernails.

O. D. D.

You told me I should do it –
that when the time was right
I was to push you
from the height of Beachy Head.

The time has always been
just as right or wrong, as it has
and ever will be.
I now question whom it is you plan

to be setting free?
I can push but you will pull
and the continuum of the reverse
is forever the inevitable lack

of release for either you or me.
But what I do know
is that you'll never find
the bones to jump.

Dalliance   (*After John Ashbury*)

There is no *I* in team
when hanging out
with Bedouins, kicking
footballs. Who left the rice to overcook?
We don't score
like that, right?   Deal left

Someone is typing a comment

Another blooper from Ally & Mr. Coco.
It seems to be that people are supporting
WMHD by writing
Amazing Public Statements.
So here is yours: I have Agoraphobia
but I'm writing this outside.

Who likes this?

(I) can always rely on friends
to keep me upbeat and motivated.
Who said 'Thank you?' and somebody else tell me

why pockets on clothing aren't always pockets.

Someone Is Typing…

Watch yerself, cunt. I got one more
round left in me.
                              Fuck toast –
holed up

trying not to look too dodgy
these poems shimmer.
Slash them. Already memories hidden
under the bed.

Who can see I already seen this?

Poetry is my favourite sin.
First draft of old street, new town.
Leaf-puppets are so extraordinarily wonderful.
He goes off to get seriously arsed
by rats. Maybe you just don't get it
what with you being a man.

Who balances a satellite of snot on their shoulders?
When is gin and vermouth available
on prescription? Dogs chase geese.

Who is not laughing their fucking arse off?

Global warming is not humanity
nor Co2, it is that same man's flaccid
approach to everything.
Trump is not a card game but a longing
to go live with grandma.

> *I am now a MILF*
> *this subversive 'gratitude'*
> *can go fuck itself.*

Part 3

Two Roads Home

I run dry of ink the moment
you turn sharp left. The junction
that split us in to two; directions
on my Sat Nav claw you back home
and me, to a lion pit where their snarls
serve as nothing but distraction
from the rear-view mirror and the indicator
that disappears to your wife – leaving me
alone. I up the radio and sing.

The Mistress

I don't mind you lying
in my bed – the afternoon pouring
at the window until dusk draws
in blankets across your chest.
I am not your wife
notifying a muted phone. I don't
wash your guilt-ridden clothes
or avoid the look
you are unable to hide.
I don't trade my flesh
for weekend chores or keep
tally on your ubiquitous
bank records. This evening
as you rehearse your story
I will collect her evidence
from these empty rooms
I call 'home'.

Don't claim to love me
then sink into sleep as tears
soak my cheeks. Go home.

Paper Boat

I am likened to a lifeguard –
the perfect specimen: hip to hip
bone-jut icebergs from the flattened
ocean between. Ripples crease
in the space beneath my breasts.
My thighs in froth-tipped waves
the lunar pull – rhythmic tides

until you soften. Within the storm
I waste to papier-mache. Painted lips
now clown-like, veneer dredged
from the abyss. Your cardboard
cut-out figure wilts, the carving knife
shoulder-blades, rudderless
in the beach-tangle of sheets.

Orientation

I arrive and rearrange
your space: move stuff, switch
on lamps, turn off
the overhead bulb that dangles
like a hanged-man from the ceiling.
Slide a box of sugar-free muesli
between half-eaten packets
of Weetabix. Spray your sheets.
Vanish most things. Swap around
the music playlist.
Boil the kettle, for both of us
to whistle. Then silently curse
at your dairy-free fridge.
And wonder why you keep
so many bicycles in the hallway
and no clean cups on the shelves.

The Busy Mouth

You stand at the bar, a difficult twenty
creased in your palm just an hour after
your attempt to discipline my dog.

(She didn't even bother to bark).
You park your car in equidistance
from our homes, my silence breaths

the percentage proof between us.
I remember how you like to lie
at my breast like a newborn

whilst I stroke your hair to remind you
you are not strong enough
for either one of us.

*

We walk down the shops,
afterwards. Your elbow knocks mine
every second step. If I move
you move too until my coat-sleeve
snags at curious branches
peering over garden walls.

You perforate our ink-spilled dark
with threads of hot words, I do not hear.
Billowing white jets of breath
lead our pace.

In the off-license
I scan the spirit shelf
while you pay
for your own bag of crisps.

On the way back, you crunch
through the packet, without sharing
tipping the crumbs like a mini-digger
at your busy mouth.

Back at your flat, you put the kettle on
and leave it whistling for far too long.
I aim to your room, unscrew
my vodka and pour half the contents
over the freshly fucked sheets.

For Starters

You leave me to hang;
a poorly-thought-out dinner light
      feasting on the difficulties of the main course.

Drop-bulb, highlighting
hundred-watt secrets that swing between us:
stark
      white
            nowhere to hide.

I ask you
but your answers come as silence, clammed up
hard-to-split crustaceans of our sin.

Fuck you
      in your retreat;
            my bed.

Between the cotton sheets washed of every remnant
      your seafood fingers
            are not wanted here.

Re-Decorating

I stare at the splatter of you across the ceiling
like reflections of the splintered veins sketched

in the whites of my eyes. The knife still lies
where we found it: untouched; a congealed mass –

the final remnants of us. The room wreaks
of rusty nails, damp towels and local anaesthetic.

My mind looks like binary code – punched
lashes weighed down with dissidence and salt.

No matter how many sky-blue gowns scrub
themselves free of my skin, I am convinced

that this fractal expression of your protest
was somehow not everyone else's fault.

Behind Closed Doors

I will pet you with the mirrored indifference
I flirt with next-door's cat, avoid your breath
as it wrestles with the beads
of sweat behind my throat.

I will pretend the fingers that prickle
at my nipples, belong
to someone else's hands.
And let you part my thighs

with the ease I drew the curtains
on last night's cancelled rain –
we could have been outside.
I will smash your dreams

with silence whilst re-arranging photographs
old walls re-shined
with times I was Rapunzel.
I want to want you

with the vigour I tore my underwear
from beneath my skirt –
the night that shot like cocaine
but for now, I will kiss you

with the same empty mouth.

Scrabble

It's been a month
and you still haven't made me come.

I have a score-card
etched behind my eyes

like the scrabble game last night
when my victory of 'Visited'

was thwarted, by your triple-word reversion
to a previous condition; Withdrawal.

And then you take me back to bed
whilst my mind, hides; cheated

from the seven-letter bonus score.
You pump, like a gas station

the pen still wet behind your ear.
I bite you.

Then laugh, inwardly
at how your eyebrows curl

like a nineteen-eighties cliché
and how the hair on your back

will keep you warm this Winter
whilst I find myself

a less literate fuck.

Falling Open

You wear that morning face
as often as I wear you. No blanks
or blankets. Small scabs
stretch the piste
of your collarbone. Our edges peel.

Fingernails bear evidence
of the night. You feign
a dream – small murmurs
for small mercies. I bypass
the stairs

and turn the night over
with an open window.
Books pave the patio and I know
how hard they fell. Nobody is fooled.
Our spines ache.

The Long Walk

A funeral home lies in equidistance
from my front door and the cemetery gate.

I've measured it in Kilojoules – walked
twice from each direction and averaged

the results to take account
of the vague decline/incline en-route.

Back home, I fill a coffee cup
with water from the tap, arrange the pills

into a clown-face before pressing my tongue
at the worktop to lick him up.

Tomorrow, I may not swallow
and try to scare myself to death.

A Dissection of the Stale

I find pieces of you in the morning, stuck to the
underside
of freshly-fucked sheets and to the underwear you leave

inside out, hanging from the radiator with the authority
of a man who pays his own bills, or the boy whose
parents

have been suckers for far too long. I barely double-take
these days but replace the lids on jars, throw the debris

at the bin and slam-shut the half-hung drawers with
attitude
reminiscent of a well-kept slave. I pretend not to wait

to hear the key stutter at the latch and forget to
remember
not to laugh at your self-soothing and hide the
packaging

from the faux-fresh supper. I pay the credit card bill
before the post comes, and clear the history from my
search.

Buy Rope

wrapped as a royal blue ball
that requires too much thought
to unravel – the ends are woven
through the middle. You couldn't solve
this puzzle even if you were paid.

Ten meters now seems excessive
yet the width, too thin and frayed
You wonder if you could double
it up or if you can still remember
if need be, how to plait.

You wouldn't dream to use this
as a rope swing for the kids; those
half your weight, in every way.
It would snap with your inadequate
attempt to secure the knots.

It appears more suitable for chaffing
gagging or lacing than it does
for a hanging. Dying should be an Art
not an undeniable embarrassment
of scars. You tie it between two

fence posts and hang out
yesterday's chores; damp towels
lick the grass and the garden creeps
with wafts of vomit. When she returns
she will small-smile at your efforts

to help around the home
and ask if you remembered
to clean your teeth, make a start
on your CV, buy more loo roll
and make the cottage pie for dinner.

Last Kiss

    I promise it will shrink with time; the vision will fade
into 3am confusion and then occasional déjà vu.
    You can let go, I say, let it travel from mind
to bone. I liken it to cancer. We got through that.
    I will nurse you this time. Winter, my prognosis
will hurt but the first flush of Spring will not fail
    to lighten the load. I say too much. I always do.
I cook the same food, feign sleep on the same pillow
    my back to yours, as I monitor your every breath.
You grow a beard, I let my pubic hair grow
    We go to therapy. You take your pills.
I forget now where you said you saw it
    the kiss that split us back to two.

Mother's Work

I smell his trousers; they smell
of dog and cat and half-sucked lollipops.

But it is just his Scooby-Doo pants I chuck
at the washing machine's gaping mouth

hungry for familiar patterns.
The cling-film's end recoils from remnants of Supper

as the dishwasher spits
and swallows memories in one.

There is no bark, no cry of feline
expectation in this house; only their sweet-wrappers

stuck inside un-emptied pockets and bottoms of socks
still mismatched from organized drawers

at Daddy's. I mop sadness from each tear duct;
all attempts to drown the ties between us, coursing

through my veins. I peg us out in equal measure;
a spoonful of detergent, a slither of Sunday's breast.

I smell his trousers. They smell
of another woman's home.

We are born from one
        but the angle of the knife
                will split us in two

Packing Up

Until this morning, you've left
every trace of you too.
Sometimes, a right sock
the wrong way round
found between the crumpled mess
of linen, still warm
from your last goodbye. Kisses
worn upon me – last night's
cling-film peeling at the edges
of my tolerance. The clatter
at the front-door catch
setting my nerves to the evidence:
a hold-all, light yet filled
with everything. Still unzipped –
a week's worth of future
spilling at the seams.

The Night You Left

I threw it all
under the stairs. Angular door
shut tight. Peeling paintwork
snowflakes dancing in our quake.

*

You check yourself,
driver's seat, in the rear
view mirror. Hungry mouth
now silenced with anger.

*

I pour half a bottle
of metaphor – draining crimson
whilst Buddha hidden beneath
your shoes, can't see out.

Portrait of the Mother

Now she is gone, there is nothing but ocean
waiting to take her to vaporous shades
of flail. Bereft of her child, this mother wails
hollow as she offers herself to the welter
its choke and tightening slip-knot
of loss. Shoals wrap bones that cease to ache
but shudder beneath a grain-less dark.

Tides churn their wreckage – sink and rise
through the hours. Slow-fire air, burnt yellow
gulps in moments of continual burial.

Yet still she calls through the wake
as her body folds itself into the cold.

Legally Bound

I've lost track.
Every drawer in every cupboard
looks the same – a chaos
of bent documents, faded
creased and confused

with the evidence left of us.
Nothing could hold it all
together – I gave up on paperclips
and staples and resorted to glue
that only served to stick

the wrong bits
back together and our own hands
forced in the wrong shapes –
never to touch each-others
as if in plaster-casts.

I rip a page out
to remind me how you left:
spineless and unread.

HANNAH M. TEASDALE

In 1976, Hannah was born and 'hard-raised' in Birmingham where she was taught the Fine Art of poor decision making. 18 years later, she was 'shot' to the Soft- South-West where she put into practice all she had learned.

In recent times, now in Cambridge, she is 'Mastering' the Fine Art of unlearning.

Hannah now identifies as a work in progress; there's no guilt, shame or inadequacy attached to 'letting go'. This is Hannah's third collection – a last-ditch attempt to learn from all those poor decisions.

'I would like to express my heartfelt thanks to Josephine and Peter Lay, Black Eyes Publishing UK for all the support and guidance required to take this uncomfortable, unforgiving and uncompromising collection to print and the incredible people who have taken the time and energy to read, digest this and thus provide brutally honest quotations'

Hannah

Full Quotations

Through a series of stark, vivid snapshots this sizzling, brave work doesn't just offer glimpses of Hannah's life, but instead leads us right to the depths of humanity. In true Teasdale form, *Indelicate Sundays* deals with the difficult head on, with unflinching and admirable honesty. Yet Hannah's turn of phrase is delicate and the poems are exquisitely crafted. Hannah's poems burn with white hot intensity and buzz with the undertow of yearning. The themes of fracture and loss circle the book, bleeding through every word, yet Hannah's unbreakable spirit and strength breathe life into the darkest of times and the book leaves you feeling uplifted. This poignant insight into a tortured life will leave you breathless and reeling and stirred to the very core.

Holly Winter-Hughes

Hannah packages her trauma, vulnerability and strength into perfectly formed punches, the likes of which, you don't realise have landed, until you're knocked out. Brilliant.

Giovani Esposito

Hannah Teasdale's third collection of poetry charts a fractured life which starts when her mother announces they are leaving home. Leaving to a cold house with a 'filthy' bed a secret hobby of stealing things begins; 'my first desire to take things that aren't mine,' but 'I never take more than I feel owed.' This start of a secret compulsive shame continues through teenage years into adulthood. The young girl feels lust when she looks at a photo of her grandfather as a young man then realises her knickers are wet when he burps after dinner. The adult woman keeps a score card of how long it has been that her lover hasn't given her an orgasm and the mistress persuades her lover to get 'an eye test'. Hannah's poetry is surprisingly shocking but delicately direct. There are no happy endings. A relationship boils down to two facts; 'We go to therapy. You take your pills' and her child's trousers smell of another woman's house. Life has become a 'chaos of bent documents.' She has become a mother who has left home and is crying for her lost child.

Dr Lucy English

"If Anais Nin and Shane Meadows met at a bar to write prose and poems it may well end up like this book. An awareness of vulnerability is a strength and Hannah Teasdale expresses this with power and insight whilst creating an urban cinematographic vibe of working-class life without for one moment feeling sorry for itself or filing itself under a label. I also respected the straight talking yet structured poems like Glass Eyes and Untouched and how Teasdale doesn't give a shit about avoiding the parallels of exploitation versus the innocence of a sexual and emotional awakening from child to adolescent to woman/human."

Anthony Owen

A straight-talking, direct and utterly beautiful collection from a poet confronting the hard realities and joyous dreams of contemporary human existence. Teasdale navigates an eventful journey from child to adulthood in all its ambiguity and shock. Shot through with violence, tension, tenderness and love, her poems don't shy away from examining the beauty, terror and often difficult outcomes of decisions taken. Connections are made and broken, relationships soar and strain, secrets are hidden and laid bare. Teasdale faces the consequences head-on, and we are caught up in the force of her thoughts - whether trying to make sense of death as a child, how sex changes the dynamics between adults, or considering the stance of the 'other' woman in a relationship with a married man. *Indelicate Sundays* is a collection that is by turns unsettling and surprising, rooted as it is in a questioning world of childhood dreams and nightmares, and adult fantasies. Yet Teasdale's poetic voice is one of surety and celebration. She is unafraid to draw on aspects of her life to speak to us all, and we are carried along with her in solidarity and wry recognition. The poems revealingly hark back and career forward, in a striking and unexpected style that is enlightening and immensely satisfying. It is no understatement to say that "these poems shimmer".

Sara-Jane Arbury